Let's Grow!

by
Maya Yang

NATIONAL
GEOGRAPHIC

Hampton-Brown

National Geographic and the Yellow Border are registered trademarks of the National Geographic Society.

National Geographic School Publishing
Hampton-Brown
www.NGSP.com

Printed in the USA.
Quad Graphics, Leominster, MA

ISBN: 978-0-7362-7990-1

18 19   10 9

Acknowledgments and credits continue on the inside back cover.

You can water the bush.

I can water the tree.

You can dig the carrots.

I can dig the onions.

You can pick the apples.

I can pick the pears.

I can grow fruits and vegetables!